Greek Mythology

*A Guide to Greek Gods,
Goddesses, Monsters, Heroes,
and the Best Mythological Tales*

Table of Contents

Introduction

Thank you for taking the time to pick up this book on Greek Mythology!

This book covers the topic of Greek Mythology, and will recount to you some of the very best and most famous mythological tales.

At the completion of this book you will have a good understanding of Greek Mythology, and have a great appreciation for the different stories and incredible characters.

These deities once played a major role in society, before the dawn of Christianity. However, as time wore on, they were revered less and less, and a lot of people have pretty much forgotten about them.

However, their incredible stories still carry on today in some forms, and are the inspiration for many different movies, books, and common sayings that we now use regularly, such as 'Pandora's box', or 'Achilles' heel'.

You will soon discover tales about some of the most famous gods, demigods, warriors, monsters, and heroes. Inside each mythological story is contained a moral, or lesson that you can take away and learn from.

Once again, thanks for taking the time to read this book, and welcome to the amazing world of Greek mythology!

Chapter 1:
What is Greek Mythology

Greek mythology is a collection of stories handed down from generation to generation throughout Greece. Starting in Ancient Greece, these stories were of ancient deities that had a hand in every day concepts, such as the rising and setting of the sun, the different Gods and their responsibilities, and the many tales of heroes and villains. Greek mythology is a very important part of ancient culture.

Greek mythology involves many stories of heroes who are the spawn of gods, and stories of the gods themselves. These tales serve to motivate people and teach them morals. For a period of time, people worshipped the gods talked about in Ancient Greek mythology, though today this religion is for the most part not followed. However, the stories are still used to illustrate morals, and are the basis for many movies, books, and television shows.

The gods were said to be over ten feet tall, but when they walked among men they were said to shape themselves to the size of humans. According to legend, this made them almost undetectable whenever they did not want to be noticed.

There are many different tales surrounding the mystery of the gods however, and they all seem to form from one place; Mount Olympus. There are many speculations as to where Olympus is located, as it cannot be seen by mortals. Some say it is in Sicily, others say it is actually on Mount Vesuvius, and was the reason for its eruption.

In Greek mythology, there are said to be twelve major gods, and three of them are referenced as the big three. All of the gods started on Mount Olympus, and from there they went about their business, often taking residence in the temples of worship people created for them.

This is the body of myths that surround a culture, and should be respected as a deep seated part of their history. For thousands of years these stories have been passed down, with their mystique only growing. Let's dive into the world of Greek Mythology now, and learn more!

Chapter 2:
In the Beginning

Hello! And welcome to my world of Greek Mythology! In this book, you will find information on all of the Greek gods and goddesses, some of the most intriguing Greek monsters, heroes, and some of the best tales that Greek mythology has to offer. Enjoy the twists and turns as you learn about the fun, dangerous, and exciting world that is Greek Mythology!

Before we get into Greek gods and goddesses, let me tell you about how they came about. This goes way back to the dawn of time, before any of us could even fathom. There was a time before the gods and goddesses, and it was not pretty. However, to know their story you must know the past.

In the beginning, the world was a horrible place. It was the known as the Age of the Titans. This was a very bleak and unwelcome time for all involved. The few humans on earth were enslaved, and made to do tasks that no human should ever have to do. The titans were cruel and often tortured these poor innocent souls to death with the tasks they required. As a result, the human population was almost entirely wiped out. Very few were able to hide from the titans, and of those who did, many died of starvation or inclement weather conditions. Heading all of this mass destruction was none other than Kronos himself. Kronos was the leader of the titans, and he was not kind or in any way a good deity.

In the beginning of time, all the planets had living deities to represent them. The Earth's deity was known as Gaia. She fell in love with Uranus. As time wore on, she gave birth to many children. She gave birth to the titans, and also to a mythical monster type we all know well, the Cyclopes. The youngest of these children was Kronos (or Cronus). Kronos was very jealous of the power of his father, and he sought to do something about it. His time would come when he realized that his father had hidden the undesirable children (Cyclopes) in the depth of Tartarus. His mother had been under the impression that these children had died in childbirth, and Gaia was furious that she had never gotten a chance to meet these children as she had with the titans.

Gaia made a great weapon for Kronos to use to take down his father. However, his father only had one weakness. He had to be castrated to be taken down, otherwise they would not succeed in overthrowing him. Kronos along with his siblings snuck up on their father. While the other titans pretended to be in awe of their father, asking him questions and keeping him distracted, Kronos castrated his father, and threw his testicles into the sea. From his blood spilled onto the earth, the Gigantes (giants) Melia (nymphs) and Erinyes (furies) were created, and from his testicles hitting the sea, Aphrodite was born. (More on her later).

Kronos took his father's place, and everything was great for awhile. There was no immorality, as Kronos started out as a just leader, but there were no laws, so eventually things started to go bad. The titans realized that the tiny creatures known as humans were very afraid of them. They didn't have any communication skills whatsoever, and looked kind of like monkeys. The titans used these creatures to do their bidding. Once they realized how weak these creatures were, they decided they needed help toughening up. The titans tortured the humans, and made them undertake tasks that were way beyond their physical capabilities. The titans felt that they were doing this race a favor, but they almost wiped them out in the process. They survived only by some humans wising up and going into hiding.

Kronos ruled with Rhea, his sister, and they were the King and Queen. They re-imprisoned the Cyclopes, and had a dragon guard them. However, Kronos's rule would soon be threatened as he was prophesied to be overthrown by his children as he had overthrown his father. He was so afraid of losing power, that when Rhea started bearing children for him, he swallowed them. He wanted to make sure that he would never be overthrown. Rhea finally had enough of his horrible behavior, and when she was pregnant with a son, Zeus, she tricked Kronos, by giving him a stone wrapped in cloth, which Kronos swallowed, thinking that it was his child. However, Zeus was alive and well, living with his grandmother, Gaia. When he reached adulthood, Zeus cut his siblings out of his father. Being immortal, they were alive, and had reached adulthood as well. Kronos was wounded, but not dead. Zeus had the Cyclopes forge his thunderbolts, Hades's helm, and Poseidon's trident. The other siblings, Demeter, Hera and Hestia (The females) went into hiding.

A long battle ensued, as Zeus and his brothers fought to overthrow the titans. Eventually they succeeded, and Kronos and most of his brothers were imprisoned in Tartarus. The other titans, that conceded defeat without a fight, such as Prometheus, Oceanus, and Atlas, were all given tasks to do. Atlas was required to hold up the world, Oceanus was to guard the sea, and Prometheus, was to guide the skies. However, even though things were calm, they were not perfect. Gaia was so enraged that Zeus had imprisoned all of her children, that she bore a child with Tartarus. This child was named Typhon. There will be more on him later in this book.

So there you have it folks. The gods and goddesses came from somewhere, and now you know where. And if you are wondering what ever happened to old Kronos, well he is still said to be trapped in the pit of Tartarus, chopped up and entombed in a magical casket to prevent him from escaping.

Chapter 3:
Gods and Goddesses of Greek Mythology

There are said to be many gods and goddesses now, and they all control certain aspects of the world we live in, even today, according to mythology. These deities have a hand in everything from the wind to wine. They all have a story, and they are all very unique, but they all are combined in a winding wraparound web of wonders. These wonderful mythological beings will open your eyes to a world entirely different from what you thought you knew.

Here is a list of the different gods and goddesses, and a little about each of them.

The Big Three

- [ ] **Zeus**

- [ ] Zeus is the King of the Gods, King of Mount Olympus, and the youngest of his siblings. However, he is also referred to as the oldest, because his siblings had to be regurgitated to experience life. He is the god of thunder and lightning, which is fitting, because his symbol is his lightning bolt weapon that he used in the defeat of Kronos. Born of Rhea and Kronos, he was hidden away and raised by his grandmother Gaia, who he later angered by imprisoning all of her children.

  He was a little bit of a playboy to be honest. He was married to Hera, but that did not keep him faithful, despite her vengeful nature. He was known to have slept with the Titaness Dione, siring Aphrodite, named after the Sea Nymph born of Uranus's downfall. He also sired many other gods, goddesses and heroes. Ares, Hebe, and Hephaestus were born to him by Hera, and many others were born to him by various other women. The gods and goddesses were Apollo, Artemis, Athena, Persephone, Dionysus, the Muses and Hermes. He also sired heroes of all shapes and sizes, the most well know of which is probably Hercules, but among others were Perseus, Minos, and Helen of Troy. He probably had a lot of other demigod children that no one knew about, as eventually he made a pact that the big three should not sire any demigod children. A prophecy arose that a child of the blood of a big three god and a human would cause the earth to either flourish, or to shatter, and the big three did not want to take the chance of the earth shattering. Though of course, they had their worldly urges, and there have been tales of other children being sired of the big three. Hades is said to have twins, a boy and a girl, Poseidon a son, and Zeus, another daughter. There are also rumored to be more that no one knew of because they never made it to their teenage years.

☐ **Hades**

☐ God of the Underworld. King of Death. Hades is another god of that makes up the big three. He is not represented in Olympus. The legends have it that the big three drew lots for the realms that they would rule over to avoid one god getting too much power. Zeus got the sky, Poseidon got the sea, and Hades got the underworld, or as we know it today, Hell. Hades was angry with his result and tried to overthrow his brothers. He was almost successful as he had managed to get Zeus's thunderbolt, and merge it with his helm, however, Poseidon struck him with his trident, before kicking him into the realm of the underworld where he was to spend his eternity. He is not represented in many tales, however one famous one speaks of the underworld quite well. Orpheus in the Underworld was an invigorating tale that involved Hades and the underworld. However, he is the least mentioned in all of Greek mythological literature. When Zeus arranged Mount Olympus, he did not leave a seat for Hades, sealing his fate as unwelcome by his family. As time wore on, however, Hades made an appearance occasionally in Olympus, and finally, a seat was added for him, though it was very rarely occupied.

☐ Poseidon

☐ The middle brother of the big three. He is the god of the sea. King of the water. His offspring, whether god or demigod, are said to be able to heal any of their injuries in water, even fatal ones. He was said to be the father of horses as well. Poseidon was known to consort with nymphs, often siring Cyclopes children. He also has been known to cause earthquakes when angry. He along with Hades often kept to himself. He is seen in a few legends, such as the one where he was such a big presence in the city of Athens (a gift to Athena) that she decided to hold a competition to see who the Athenians would choose as their patron. Each god had to give the Athenians a single gift, and then they would choose who they wanted in their city. Poseidon gifted a glorious fountain, but Athena gifted them an olive tree. The Athenians chose the olive tree as it served three purposes. Poseidon was so furious that he flooded the city, creating a large body of salt water across what was the Attic Plain. Another legend, in the time of the battle of Troy, Poseidon and Apollo rebelled against Zeus, and were temporarily stripped of their godly powers, and sent to earth as mere mortals to build the walls of Troy. When Zeus did not reward them as promised, Poseidon attacked Troy with a giant sea monster that Hercules later killed.

Goddesses

☐ **Hera**

☐ The wife of Zeus, goddess of women, families, and children. Not a whole lot is known about her other than that she is the queen of fertility, and that she was known to be very vengeful on her husband's lovers, and even on mortals who crossed her. She was also one of the children swallowed by Kronos, when the titans ruled the earth.

☐ **Persephone**

☐ Also known as Kora, the goddess of harvest, and queen of agriculture. She became the wife of Hades by means of kidnapping. Hades saw her and fell instantly in love with her. He kidnapped her and dragged her back into the underworld where he held her captive.

The story of Persephone's kidnapping is quite scandalous, as no other god had managed to steal Persephone away from her direly protective mother. In the legend, Demeter was so worried that no one would be good enough for her beautiful daughter that she hid her away from all the gods, and only let her spend time with Artemis and Athena, the two goddesses that she trusted. However, Hades had fallen in love with

Persephone from afar, and with Zeus's permission, he opened up the ground around Persephone, and brought her down to the underworld with him. Demeter was so depressed when her daughter disappeared that she neglected the world. Zeus demanded that Hades return Persephone to Demeter at once. Hades however was not going to do so without some trickery. He fed Persephone some pomegranate seeds that came from the underworld itself. This sealed her fate in having to spend at least one third of every year in the underworld with him.

Persephone herself is a formidable goddess capable of ruining the life of people who cross her. She is the goddess of vegetation, and often ruined the crops of mortals who failed to worship her when she walked the earth among them. In the underworld, she would destroy the soul of any being that dared to speak her name, thus acknowledging that she was stuck in her dreaded prison with her husband that she was forced to be with.

☐ **Athena**

☐ Athena is the goddess of wisdom and battle strategy. She was one of the more beautiful goddesses. Born of Zeus alone, but claimed as a daughter by Hera, she is a genius goddess, and was said to have never taken on a serious lover. Athena was said to be the 'virgin' goddess of the twelve, as she never got married, though Hephaestus tried to woo her several times with many trinkets made in his forge.

Not much is known about Athena, as she mainly focused on protecting her soldiers in battle. The only legend she is a main character in that is widely known is the story of Poseidon in Athens. This goddess is a calm, kind, but stern ruler of her people, and is worshiped by the highest minds in ancient Greece.

☐ Hestia

☐ The oldest Goddess, and sister of the big three, daughter of Kronos. She was known as the goddess of the hearth, and the warmth in a home. She was one of the three virgin goddesses in Olympus, Athena and Artemis being the other two.

All that is really known about Hestia is that she was a tranquil goddess, and eventually, she was replaced in the twelve gods of Olympus by Zeus's son Dionysus, as he was seemingly more willing to fight to keep Zeus in power. Hestia refused to take sides on anything, so she was cast down to be a lower level goddess.

☐ Artemis

☐ The goddess of the moon. The hunting queen, the curator of silver. The deity with the silver hair. Artemis was the desire of many men, but was conquered by none. She relied only on herself, and stayed pure, never knowing the love of a man, and never creating any offspring as well. She is known to be the huntress and the twin sister of Apollo, the god of the sun chariot. She is known to help protect virgins from rape, and help the hunters see better at night, by giving them the light of the moon.

☐ Hebe

☐ The youngest child of Zeus and Hera, she is the goddess of youth and eternal beauty. She was said to have never aged, and is the push behind some people looking so healthy in their older years. Those people are said to have lived in a way that was pleasing to her, and she blessed them with youth. She is not a very well known goddess, as she did not play a big role in Greek mythology, other than gracing women with youthful skin.

☐ Nemesis

☐ True to her name, she is the goddess of retribution. She was meant to keep the balance between human affairs. She was never known to let her own vendetta cloud her judgment, unlike other deities around her. She is not mentioned in a lot of stories, and where she is the mentioned it is only fleeting. She is a goddess of justness.

☐ Leto

☐ The Goddess of motherhood and mother to Artemis and Apollo. She was dishonored as Zeus's lover, but once her children were born, she was avenged as they became prevalent in Olympus. That is about all that is known about her as she is not an Olympus god.

☐ Aphrodite

☐ Probably the most well known Goddess, she is the goddess of beauty and love. She is said to be the most beautiful creature to ever grace mythology, and in fear of her starting a war among gods, Zeus married her to

Hephaestus, the ugliest god there was. However, she fell in love with Ares, god of war, and they had a long and torrid affair.

☐ Demeter

☐ Demeter was the daughter of Kronos, sister to Zeus, and mother to Persephone. She was kind of a lone wolf. There are not many stories about her that don't involve her daughter Persephone. She was the Goddess of harvest and grain, and Queen of the changing seasons. She did not stay confined to Olympus, and was often in one of the many temples of those who worshipped her. She was very protective of her daughter, and even went to extreme lengths as to try to hide her. She also nearly destroyed the earth when she was kidnapped by Hades. This is one goddess you would not want to cross.

Gods

☐ Ares

☐ The god of war. King of the axe. Often depicted as a rough man with a long beard. This god is said to have had a torrid affair with Aphrodite. However, in the ancient times, he was seen as a beardless youth, too soft faced for being the deity of bloodshed and violence it would seem. He once tried to steal Hades' helm of invisibility, and was almost destroyed for it. Only after pledging his services to Zeus was he spared, for which Hades was furious, as he wanted Ares destroyed.

☐ Apollo

☐ This is the king of the sun chariot, god of the arts and healing. He is the twin brother of Artemis and the son of Leto. He never got married, but had many different lovers in his time. Depicted with a toned physique, and long flowing hair, he was often fawned over by mortals and goddesses alike.

Apollo is not in many myths, but he once rebelled against Zeus with Poseidon. He was stripped of his power and sent to build the wall of Troy. He also was mentioned in the tale of Jason and the Golden Fleece, where Jason was sent to retrieve the golden fleece that was created by Apollo that possessed healing capabilities. It was said to be able to heal and ailment, and could even bring someone from death, as long as they had only just died. He is also said to drive Helios down to the other side of the earth as Helios has a hard time moving himself as he gets older and more tired. Apollo was put in charge of driving his sun chariot and keeping the sun moving.

☐ Dionysus

☐ Also known as Bacchus, Dionysus is the god of wine and fruitfulness. He is the son of Zeus and Dione. He replaced Hestia in the court of the gods, as he was more willing to take sides. Dionysus was a just god, and merely wanted to fill every home with plenty of wine to keep them in good health. However, if a mortal crossed him, he would turn their wine into water.

This punishment came back to haunt him however, when Dionysus had a torrid affair with a sea nymph that Zeus took a liking to. Zeus decided to use his own trick against him, and from that moment on, any wine that Dionysus tried to consume turned into water. It was a torture for him, and he gladly would have given up his seat on the council to be able to enjoy wine again.

☐ Hephaestus

☐ The god of forges and fire, he was the son of Hera alone, and he was born so deformed that she cast him off of Mount Olympus in a hope to kill him. She did not succeed, and he was taken in and given refuge by Poseidon, once it was seen that he had a knack for forging. Hephaestus is often depicted with the Cyclopes he instructed on forging things, as that was what he spent his time doing. He is also known as the god of fire and volcanoes, as he used the lava to harden his tools beyond that of mortal capabilities.

Hephaestus was mentioned in the tale of Achilles, as he fashioned an armor that was impenetrable to any blade that could be made, however, the armor had one catch. Hephaestus could not cover the right heel, as the armor would shatter every time, hence the term Achilles heel.

☐ Hermes

☐ The messenger god. He is often depicted wearing winged sandals, and could travel at the speed of sound. He fathered many demigod children, as he had a thing for the mortal women. He also was the god of travelers, known to help out a lost person wandering in a dangerous area, all they had to do was call out to him, no catch.

Hermes often brought on the wrath of Zeus but was too essential to the court to dispose of, so Hermes, the mischievous god that he was, kept on pushing buttons. He often slept with women that Zeus fancied, knowing that Zeus could do nothing about it but get angry.

There you have it, the list of Greek gods and goddesses and a little information about them. Some of them are more prevalent than others, and some are only fleetingly mentioned in Greek mythology.

Chapter 4:
Monsters and Creatures of Greek Mythology

This chapter will cover the most prevalent monsters and creatures mentioned in Greek Mythology, and provide some information about them.

Monsters and creatures of Greek mythology will leave you looking at everyday animals wondering why they are so plain. They are majestic, dangerous, and oh so alluring.

Monsters

☐ **Typhon**

☐ Remember this creature being mentioned earlier as the offspring of Gaia and Tartarus? He comes back into play here. He was born out of vengeance, causing him to be horrifying to look at, and even worse in temperament. He was lawless, and did not care who he hurt. He had shoulders that had hundreds of snakes growing from them, and fire that sprouted from their heads. He also had four tentacles for legs that slithered across the ground like serpents in the night. He had no language, and many at the same time. He was chaos embodied. He was as big as a mountain, and stronger than one too. The world cowered at the mention of his name. He was vile and cruel, and the worst part is, he reproduced.

Typhon decided one day to challenge Zeus for the ruling of the cosmos, however he lost tragically. He fought his hardest, but one strike from the thunderbolt that Zeus is best known for, and he went crashing down to earth in a fiery ball, completely and utterly destroyed, and then cast into the depths of Tartarus.

☐ Echidna

☐ Half woman, half snake, all evil. She was the wife to Typhon and the final daughter of Gaia, sired by Tartarus. She was the mother to Cerberus, the three headed dog, the Gorgon sisters (Medusa and her siblings) the Hydra, and the Chimera. Not much is known about her other than her birthing all of these creatures, and that when Typhon was killed by Zeus, she and her offspring were spared to keep challenging the demigods that were born, to weed out the weak ones.

☐ Hydra

☐ The Hydra is a multi-headed being surrounded by a lot of mystery. It shows up in different tales of heroes, but no two accounts are the same.

☐ The basics known about the Hydra though, is that it generally starts out with three heads, and is a type of lizard serpent creature that likes to eat humans. If you chop off one of its heads, two (or three) more grow back in its place. The only ways to destroy it is to stab it through its heart by driving a sword through its shoulder blades, which isn't easy, considering it has multiple heads. Or you can chop off all of its heads and singe the necks before they grow back. Not many people survived the hydra alone due to this.

Some legends say that though the hydra is fast and has many heads and can sense a man for miles away using its tongue, it is blind and deaf.

☐ Cerberus

☐ The three headed dog that guards the underworld. Legend says that Echidna birthed Cerberus, a three headed dog like creature that stood ten feet tall. He was fierce looking, but was soft, and no amount of torture would make him mean. Echidna cast him out, when Hades found him, and brought him into his realm and made him a protector. Hades trained Cerberus to stop escapees, rather than trying to make him mean.

☐ Orthrus

☐ Brother of Cerberus. When Cerberus turned out to be a gentle giant, Echidna tried to make another one of him, thus creating Orthrus. He was a strong two headed dog like creature who was a little meaner, and was used to guard the cattle of Greyson, but he was later killed by Hercules.

☐ Gorgon Sisters

☐ These three were sisters that wreaked havoc upon the world. There are two myths surrounding them, and many argue over which one is correct. Some say that they were born to Typhon and Echidna, and others say that they were born to Phorcys and Ceto of the western setting sun. However, the second pair is more widely known, so we will stick with that myth for right now. In this myth, there were three sisters, and they were horrid looking creatures with dragon like scales and wings. The oldest was Stheno, or Strength. Euryale, or Wide Leaping. Medusa, or Queen. Medusa was the only one who was not immortal, but was the only one who could turn any being into stone when she glanced at them. She was eventually defeated by Perseus with the help of Athena.

☐ The Gray Ones

☐ These three sisters were the sisters of the Gorgons. They were of a gray pallor, and shared one eye and one tooth. They guarded the gorgon sisters until Perseus stole their eye and tooth, forcing them to tell him where they were.

☐ Minotaur

☐ This half bull, half man beast has a thirst for human blood. They are often found chasing demigods, especially ones that have been rumored to be sired by one of the big three. They stand eight feet tall, and have horns as long as a mans arm. To destroy them you have to cut off their own horn and stab them in the heart with it.

☐ The Nymph

☐ These can be kind, or they can be evil. They are beautiful maidens that ensnare the hearts of men. For gods, they will do anything, but they often lure mortal men into their caves, and kill them to devour.

☐ **Sirens**

☐ These creatures you have probably heard about before. They lure sea men to their caves by singing a beautiful song that entrances them, causing them to wreck on the island and die. Then the sirens devour the sea men and other people crossing the ocean. They are a type of nymph that can shape shift into your deepest desires.

There are some creatures and monsters for you to marvel over. They are found in many different forms of mythology. They are necessary to keep the balance between good and evil.

Chapter 5:
Heroes and Their Tales

There are many different heroes in Greek mythology. Pick up a book by Homer, and you will see that these heroes tales are not fairy tales either. There are many other tales that are passed down from generation to generation, and some have even made it into kids shows, such as Hercules. There are many movies on heroes of godly lineage as well, however, as time goes on they get fewer and fewer. Maybe that is because all of the good tales have been told over and over again, and there is no new ways for them to be portrayed. However, this is causing Greek mythology to slowly slide away from the minds of the people, and that is a horrible thing, as if it is forgotten, it will mean the destruction of the culture.

So hopefully these tales will ignite your interest in learning more about Greek mythology, and will inspire you to share this book with your friend. Because there is nothing better than sharing a great thing with your friend, and watching them enjoy something new, and it is even better when you can enjoy it together.

The Heroes

Hercules

Let us start with one of the most prevalent heroes in western knowledge, Hercules. He was the son of Zeus, born to a mortal woman whom he fancied. This woman went by the name of Alcmene, and she was beautiful.

Hercules was raised to be a hero. From the time he could walk, he was trained to be strong. He had regular visits from his father Zeus, and was very close to his mother. He was kind, and handsome, and many women tried to win his heart, but his heart was in the battle. He was stronger than any mortal man could dream to be, and he was faster as well.

Eventually, he fell in love however, despite being told he should not. He was smitten by a fair maiden, and with her he sired five beautiful children, and Hercules was happy. However, Hera was displeased with his disobedience, and drove him mad. He killed his wife and children in their sleep one night.

Once his mind had cleared, he had become horrified at what he had done. He went to his king, and begged for penance. The king purified him, and the sent him to the Oracle of Delphi, who told him that the only way he could be forgiven, was to survive twelve tasks, known as labors.

These labors were not easy. They were designed to kill Hercules. Here are the tasks:

☐ 1. Kill the Nemean Lion

☐ This was a gold, giant lion, the offspring of Typhon. It would transform into a wounded soldier and lure women into his lair. He would then devour these women. Many tried to slay him, but they were unable to, because his hide was impervious to mortal blades. Many died in an attempt to extradite this beast. Hercules was sent to kill it. He wandered for days, until coming upon its cave. At first he tried to kill it with arrows, but upon finding its hide impenetrable, he decided on a more one on one approach with the lion.

Blocking off one entrance to the cave after the lion entered, he entered the other entrance, and snuck up on the lion. He then used his immense strength to strangle it to death.

☐ **2. Kill the Lernean Hydra**

☐ As was explained earlier, the Hydra was a foul beast that had the magical properties to make it grow all of its heads back when destroyed. Hercules was to kill one with nine heads. This hydra was raised up by Hera herself to kill Hercules. Hercules was not able to do this alone though. He called upon a cousin to help him slay the Hydra. After he cut off the heads, his cousin cauterized them. However, the Hydra had one immortal head. Hercules removed this head with a gold blade gifted to him by Athena. After he killed the Hydra, he made arrows dipped in its poisonous blood for further endeavors.

☐ **3. Capture the Ceryneian Hind**

☐ This is a type of deer that is considered sacred to Artemis. This was a task that was designed to cause the goddess to destroy Hercules, as no man or beast seemingly could. Hercules tracked this beast for a year, before finally capturing it in a trap net while it was sleeping. Artemis stopped him then, preparing to destroy the man who defiled her precious beast. However, Hercules pleaded forgiveness, promising to return it once he had proven to the king he had captured it. Artemis agreed. The king wanted to keep the deer, so Hercules told him that he could have it if he came and took it from him. However, as soon as Hercules let it go, the deer sprinted off at lightning speed back to its mistress, and thus Hercules completed his third task.

☐ 4. Catch the Erymanthian Boar

☐ This task contained many twists and turns, and was not really about catching the boar at all, though this boar was no regular boar. Bigger than most men, it was lightning fast, and super strong. Hercules was ordered to capture it, and bring it back alive.

☐ On his way to finding the boar, he stopped by a cave. In this cave lived a Centaur by the name of Pholus. Pholus and Hercules dined, and then they shared a barrel of wine with the other centaurs. However, the centaurs did not know that wine straight from Dionysus had to be tempered with water, and they became quite drunk, and attacked Hercules. Hercules killed many with his poison arrows, and even accidentally struck Pholus and the immortal Chiron. Chiron was in so much pain that he begged to take over Prometheus's torture of having his liver eaten daily, thus to have the poison removed from his system. Hercules then killed the eagle that was torturing Chiron, and in return, Chiron advised him on how to capture the boar. Once Hercules returned with the boar, the king was so frightened by it that he hid and demanded for it be killed.

☐ 5. Clean the Augean Stables

☐ This was designed to humiliate Hercules, and be nigh on impossible. The cattle were healthy and immortal, and produced more dung than any mortal cow. The stables had sat un-cleaned for over thirty years, and housed a thousand cattle. Hercules was promised a third of the cattle if he cleaned the stables in one day, as King Augeus felt it was not possible. Hercules rerouted two rivers to wash away the dung and muck, and get the stables clean. After Augeus denied the payment, and was taken to court, he banished both Hercules and his son who supported Hercules. Hercules later returned and slayed Augeus, and gave the kingdom to his son. When he returned back, his king rebuked his success saying that since he was paid for it, and the rivers did the work for him, he did not get to count this labor as a success.

☐ 6. Defeat the Stymphalian Birds

☐ Hercules was sent to rid a town of evil birds that were a favorite of Ares. These birds had poisonous dung, and metal beaks that tore through human flesh without a problem. They had completely ruined the town, and the few that survived were left with no crops, and were suffering a massive famine. Hercules killed them with some more of his poison arrows, and the ones that he didn't kill flew away never to return.

☐ 7. Cretan Bull

☐ Once again, Hercules had to capture a beast. This time it was the bull that had been wreaking havoc on Crete. He sailed to Crete, and was given permission to remove the bull. He snuck up behind it, and throttled the creature, stopping when it had just lost consciousness. He shipped it to his king, and the king ordered it to be sent away. It wandered to the city of Marathon, and later was known as the Marathon bull.

☐ 8. Capture the Mares of Diomedes

☐ These mares were not docile horses. They were trained to eat human flesh and they shot fire out of their mouths. Hercules cut their ties and scared them onto a peninsula. He dug a trench around it very quickly, and it filled with water, making it an island. When Diomedes came to fetch his horses, Hercules killed him and fed him to the horses. After the horses ate, they calmed down enough for Hercules to tie their mouths shut and take them back to the king.

☐ 9. Retrieve the Belt of Hippolyta

☐ Hercules was ordered to retrieve the belt of Hippolyta. This was given to her by Ares. He planned to woo Hippolyta, and it would have gone well had it not been for Hera. She disguised herself as she walked among the mortal women and told them that Hercules was planning to carry the queen off. They confronted Hercules, and he was convinced that this was Hippolyta's plan the entire time, and killed her. He took the belt and went back home.

☐ 10. Obtain the Cattle Geryon

☐ This was not an easy task as he had to travel very far, and get past their guard Orthrus, the two headed brother of Cerberus. He also had to get past the shepherd and Geryon himself. He killed the dog with one blow from a club, and the shepherd was killed the same way. He killed Geryon with a poison arrow before finally driving the cattle back to the king.

☐ 11. Steal the Apples of Hesperides

☐ Hercules had to steal the magical apples of Hesperides. To do this he captured the old man of the sea. The old man of the sea told him where to find the apples. Once he was almost there, he found himself blocked by the immortal Antaeus. However, Antaeus was only immortal if he touched the earth. Hercules killed him by lifting him up and crushing him with his immense strength. Finally, he arrived at the gardens where Atlas was holding up the heavens. Hercules offered to take his place for a while. In exchange, Atlas went and got him some apples, as he was the father of the Hesperides. Atlas did not want to take the heavens back, but Hercules tricked him by asking Atlas to hold them for just a moment longer while he adjusted his cloak. Once Atlas once again was under the heavens, Hercules fled with the apples.

☐ 12. Capture Cerberus

☐ This one was supposed to be an impossible task for Hercules, but it turned out to be one of the easiest. Hercules entered the Underworld guided by Athena and Hermes. Upon entrance, he was met by Hades. Hades, amused by his plight agreed to let Hercules take Cerberus if he could tame him without any weapons. Hercules knocked the dog out with his brute strength and carried him back home. His king was frightened by the dog so much, that he begged Hercules to take the dog back to Hades, and told Hercules that he was free from any further labors.

Perseus

Perseus was born to Danae who was imprisoned by her father Acrisius. Acrisius was fearful of the fact that he was to be overthrown by her son, and thus tried to keep Danae childless. Zeus appeared to her in a shower of gold, and impregnated her. Argos cast Danae and her child out to sea rather than killing them for fear of bringing on the wrath of Zeus. They washed up on the shore of Serifos, where Perseus grew up.

As he reached adulthood, he realized that the king of Serifos had fallen for his mother, and when challenged, the king devised a plan to rid of Perseus. He offered a banquet, and required attendance, and required that you gift him a horse to offer to the gods. Perseus did not have a horse to give, and offered that the King name a gift, and he would not refuse. Polydectes, the king, requested Medusa's head.

Medusa was the only mortal of the three Gorgon sisters. This mortality was due to her own transgressions. She was said to be the beautiful one of the sisters, as the other two were hideous. However, she angered Athena, by laying with Poseidon in her temple. Athena made her mortal, and replaced her beautiful hair with hundreds of snakes.

Perseus was instructed to find the Hesperides. He came across the Graeae, or Gray Ones. When they refused to help him find the Hesperides, he stole the one eye and tooth that they shared, and would not return it until they helped him. Upon getting the answers that he needed, he returned the tooth and eye, and continued on his way. He was given a blade to kill the Gorgon with, a knapsack in which to keep her head, the helm of invisibility, winged sandals, and a polished shield. Perseus snuck up on the Gorgon using the shield to catch her reflection, and then beheaded her. He used the helm of invisibility to disappear without a trace as the other sisters chased him.

Perseus did not have many side quests other than killing Acrisius. He had a few adventures along the way, but never killed his grandfather on purpose. There are many different tales as to how Acrisius died.

Achilles

Achilles was not a god spawn, but he was the spawn of a Nereid, a Sea Nymph. This gave him special abilities compared to that of a mere mortal. His mother was the desire of both Zeus and Poseidon, until they were warned that Thetis would bear a son stronger than Kronos. To prevent this, they had her marry a mortal king, Peleus.

There are three myths surrounding Achilles. One that he was immortal by being dipped in the river Styx, but was left vulnerable at his heel because that was where his mother held him. Another is that his mortal parts were burned away by his mother, but she was interrupted by his father, before he was completely through, leaving his heel vulnerable. The third is that he was not invulnerable, but Hephaestus made him armor, but could not get the steel to bend at the heel without shattering.

Achilles was very important in the Trojan war. He was strong, invulnerable, and had a rage that never went away. He was the bane of the Trojans existence, as they could not defeat the Greeks with this man at their lead. However, he would not be their problem forever.

Achilles was a very vengeful man, and when Menmon killed his best friend, he got revenge, but Menmon was the son of a goddess, and that goddess sent a man named Paris, Menmon's cousin, to avenge Menmon's death. Paris hid in a bush, knowing that facing Achilles would spell his death. He took a marked shot with a poison arrow, striking Achilles in his heel. Achilles fell, never to rise again.

The term Achilles heel is often used today to reference a weakness that we possess. This term is the result of this mythological tale!

Chapter 6:
Pandora's Box

According to myth, Pandora was the first woman on earth. She was created by the order of Zeus, and was formed from clay, sculpted by Hermes. There are several different versions to this story, but what follows is the most commonly told.

Pandora was created as a punishment to humankind, in response to Prometheus stealing fire and then giving it to the humans, against Zues' orders. Pandora was given gifts from each of the Gods, from beauty, to curiosity, to musical ability. These gifts formed her personality, and created a cunning and curious woman.

Pandora was also given a box, with unknown things inside; but was instructed to never open the box. The box was filled with different evil things, that should never be released onto the world – but Pandora was created with a curious manner about her, and so she struggled to restrain herself.

Hermes took Pandora to Epimetheus, the brother of Prometheus in order to have them wed. Prometheus was not in good favor with the Gods, and had advised his brother to not accept any gifts from them. Pandora's beauty however, captivated Epimetheus, and he accepted her as his wife right away.

Pandora struggled for a while to refrain from opening the box, but eventually her curiosity prevailed. When she opened the box, all of the horrors known to humankind escaped out into the world. Strife, sickness, toil, and a range of other terrors escaped the box.

Before all of the contents escaped, Pandora was able to close the box with just one thing left inside of it – hope.

The phrase 'Pandora's box' stems from this story, and is often used to describe a taking a seemingly small and innocent action that then creates a lot of problems! When we don't know how dire the consequences will be of a small action, it is as if we opened up Pandora's box.

There are several different versions of this tale. In many, the 'box' is actually referred to as a jar. The changing of the story to a 'box' only occurred in the 16th century, when it was translated to Latin. Since then, the phrase 'Pandora's box' has grown famous.

In some versions of the story, the jar or box was actually in the possession of Epimetheus already, and Pandora found it in his home.

Regardless of the exact version of events, the key components of the story remain the same. Zeus wanted to punish the humans, and did so by creating the first woman and making her overly curious, cunning, and not so trustworthy.

Chapter 7:
Trojan War

The Trojan war (also known as the battle of Troy) was a war between the people of Greece, and the people of the city of Troy.

King Priam ruled in the wealthy city of Troy. He had many children, and the future seemed very bright for the King and his family. However, one night his wife, Hecuba, had a nightmare in which she gave birth to a deadly firebrand. The seers interpreted this to mean that her unborn child would destroy Troy and its inhabitants. When the child was born, he was disposed of at Mount Ida. In the end, the child was nursed by a she-bear and managed to survive. The child grew up to be a shepherd, named Paris. Paris later on took the nymph Oenone as a lover.

At the wedding of Peleus and Thetis the gods were enjoying themselves when Eris threw a golden apple into their midst with the words, "For the fairest". Hera, Athena, and Aphrodite all tried to claim the apple as their own. An argument erupted, and they ended up up asking Zeus to judge between them and choose the fairest. Zeus refused to choose, and directed the three goddesses to a shepherd on Mount Ida who could decide who he thought was the most deserving. The shepherd was of course, none other than Paris.

The goddesses approached Paris and each tried to bribe him to select her as the fairest. Hera promised to make him a king who would rule Asia and have great wealth. Athena offered to give him wisdom and invincibility in warfare. Aphrodite was the winner however, as she offered Paris the most beautiful woman in the world - the stunning Helen. In making this choice however, Paris made powerful enemies of Hera and Athena. Both women vowed to destroy both Paris, and also the city of Troy.

On learning that he would soon be with Helen, Paris returned to Troy, where he exposed himself as a true prince, the legitimate son of Priam and Hecuba. With no further use for Oenone, he left her. Next, he sailed for Sparta. While there, he seduced Helen during her husband's absence, before returning to Troy with her.

At the same time, Paris' sister Cassandra was in trouble. Apollo gave her the gift of prophecy in an attempt to make love to her, but she had taken a vow of chastity and so, resisted him. In retribution, Apollo transformed his gift into a curse by making it so that no one would believe her prophecies. When Paris returned with Helen and stood before Priam to get his father's acceptance, Cassandra burst into the room. She prophesized that incredible suffering would be caused by her lusting brother. Of course, due to the cure, Priam did not believe this prophecy. He thought that Cassandra was mad, and had his own daughter locked in a cell.

When Menelaus returned to Sparta and found that his wife Helen had abandoned him for Paris, he summoned the Greek leaders, and together they set off to to conquer Troy and recover Helen. These leaders were all pledged to aid Menelaus, and so did not hesitate to join his cause. Thus Paris' actions started the Trojan War, which would ultimately fulfill the prophetic dream his mother had of giving birth to a firebrand that would eventually lead to the destruction of Troy.

The Greek chieftains assembled at Aulis under the leadership of Agamemnon, the brother of Menelaus. The majority of the warriors were enthusiastic about the journey, and were eager to burn and destroy Troy. However, not all in Greece were wanting to join the cause.

Odysseus was told by an oracle that he would be away from home for 20 years if he went on the journey, and so he pretended to be overcome with madness when the Greek leaders came to recruit him. Palamedes exposed the act, and Odysseus was forced to go. It would have been impossible for the Greeks to take Troy without the help of Achilles, and so the Greeks went to Scyros to recruit him. Achilles was almost completely invulnerable as a fighter, because his mother, Thetis, had dipped him in the River Styx at birth, rendering him immortal everywhere but in his heel. Achilles was tutored by Chiron, and as he grew he became an incredibly swift and fearsome warrior. He knew that he would have a short but glorious life if he went to Troy, and so he had his mother disguise him in women's clothing at the Scyrian court. However, Odysseus discovered Achilles, and he too eventually consented to go.

At first the Greeks sailed to Mysia, believing that it was Troy. Because of this mistake, they started war with the Mysians. The Mysian king, Telephus, was wounded in the battle by Achilles.

Learning of their geographical mistake, the Greeks sailed back to Aulis. Since an oracle had said that Troy could not be taken without the advice of Telephus', Achilles was obliged to heal him. The Trojan prophet, Calchas, had sided with the Greeks, and when unfavorable winds prevented the Greeks from sailing, Calchas declared that the goddess Artemis wanted the sacrifice of a virgin. Agamemnon's daughter Iphigenia was chosen and sent for under the pretext that she would marry Achilles.

Iphigenia however, willingly allowed herself to be sacrificed for the Greek cause. According to some versions of the tale though, Artemis sacrificed a deer in her place and carried her off to the land of the Taurians. In any case, the wind stopped, and the Greeks were able to continue onwards to Troy.

An oracle had prophesized that the first man to step foot onshore Trojan territory would be the first to lose their life. Protesilaus took this burden on himself, and was engaged in a losing skirmish with Hector, the Trojan prince.

Hector, a great warrior, bore the knowledge that both he and his city were doomed. If his brother Troilus had lived to be twenty years old, Troy might have been spared, but Achilles killed the boy while still in his teens. Troy did have one other defender worth noting however, Aeneas, an ally from a neighboring land. The Greek army, however, was full of heroes. There was Agamemnon, Menelaus, Nestor, Odysseus, and Achilles, along with Diomedes and the two Ajaxes.

The gods played a role in the war also, occasionally deciding the outcome of various battles. Apollo, Artemis, Ares, and Aphrodite sided with the Trojans, while Hera, Athena, Poseidon, Hermes, and Hephaestus aided the Greeks. Zeus only interfered on occasion. For the most part though he maintained neutrality.

After nine years of fighting, the Greeks had managed to destroy many kingdoms that were allies of Troy in Asia, but they had not made much progress against Troy itself. There was a lot of tension between the Greeks. Odysseus still held a grudge against Palamedes, the man who had ruthlessly shown his madness to be a hoax, forcing him to join the war. When Palamedes denounced Odysseus for taking them on an unsuccessful foraging expedition, Odysseus framed

Palamedes, making him appear as a traitor. Palamedes was stoned to death as a result.

But afterwards, and even more problematic argument occurred. This time it was between Agamemnon and Achilles. Agamemnon had taken the daughter of a priest of Apollo as a trophy of war, and when her father came to ransom her, Agamemnon sent him away without her. The priest called upon Apollo to assist him, and so Apollo sent a plague to the Greeks that killed many. Achilles called upon the council and demanded that Agamemnon give back the girl, Chryseis, to her father the priest. Agamemnon reluctantly agreed, but insisted on taking Achilles' own prize, the maid Briseis, as a replacement. This suggestion would have resulted in murder had Athena not intervened. Achilles then gave up Briseis, also decided to withdraw from the war. Since the Greek victories up to that point had been a result of Achilles' strength and ability in battle, this was a huge problem for the Greeks. Achilles told his mother, Thetis, to petition Zeus for Trojan victories, which she did.

Once they saw that Achilles and his closest comrades had withdrawn from the war, the Trojans made an attack. Agamemnon decided to grant a truce in which it was agreed that Paris and Menelaus would fight in single combat for Helen. But the duel was inconclusive, for Aphrodite, seeing that Paris was losing, wrapped him in a magic cloud and took him back to Troy.

Menelaus searched for Paris in the Trojan ranks, and Agamemnon demanded that the Trojans surrender Helen. The Trojans were willing, which possibly would have ended the war. However, Hera desperately wanted Troy destroyed, so she sent Athena to break the truce. Athena managed to persuade the Trojan archer Pandarus to fire an arrow at

Menelaus. The shot grazed Menelaus, and the fighting resumed just as it had been before.

The great Ajax and Diomedes fought in a forceful manner, killing dozens and dozens of Trojans. Diomedes killed Pandarus and wounded Aeneas. Aphrodite came to rescue her son Aeneas, but Diomedes managed to wound her wrist, causing the goddess to flee. However, Apollo retrieved Aeneas from the field and he was then cured by Artemis. Diomedes then encountered Hector, who was accompanied by the fearsome Ares, the god of battle. Diomedes was intimidated by the god, and the Greeks retreated. Athena, however gave Diomedes the courage to attack Ares. Ares was injured, and crying in pain he fled to Olympus.

Hector was forced to retreat, and was advised to return to Troy and plead to his mother Hecuba to offer her most beautiful robe in exchange for mercy from Athena. His mother agreed, but the plea failed to please the goddess. After a discussion with his wife Andromache and spending time with his infant son Astyanax, Hector went back to the field and issued a challenge to duel to Achilles, but he declined. Instead, Ajax accepted the challenge, and in the fight Ajax slightly bested Hector. The two warriors parted afterwards, and exchanged gifts as a sign of respect.

Zeus honored his promise to Thetis, who had asked him to aid the Trojans, by ordering the other gods to leave the battlefield. Consequentially, the Greeks lost badly. Under Hector's relentless assault, the Greeks were almost forced into retreat by evening. Disheartened, Agamemnon considered abandoning the siege of Troy. However, Nestor, who was old and wise, recommended that he make peace with Achilles by giving him back Briseis, and a pile of wealth to boot. Achilles listened to the proposal from Agamemnon courteously, but refused the offer. His pride was at stake, and he would only fight if he or his Myrmidons were threatened. The situation seemed hopeless. Nonetheless, that night Odysseus and Diomedes raided the Trojan camp and killed many, including King Rhesus.

The next day the Greeks were forced to retreat back to the beach where their boats were, and Agamemnon, Odysseus, and Diomedes were wounded. Hera decided that she would turn the tide of battle. Using Aphrodite's magic girdle, she seduced Zeus into making love to her and forgetting about the war. While Zeus was occupied, Poseidon returned to the battle and forced the Trojans into retreat. Ajax hurled a boulder at Hector which knocked him down, whereupon the Trojans stampeded madly for the city. Once Zeus had recovered from his infatuation, he saw the chaos and threatened to beat Hera. Once again, he also ordered Poseidon from the field.

Apollo came to Hector's aid, bringing him back to health. Once again, the Trojans gained the upper hand. With Hector in the forefront, the Trojans beat down the barricades the Greeks had put in place to protect their ships. Greatly worried, Achilles' companion Patroclus tried to persuade his friend to fight, but still Achilles refused. So instead, Patroclus borrowed Achilles' armor and entered the battle. Disguised by the armor, the Trojans thought that is was in fact Achilles who was fighting, and began to panic. Patroclus slaughtered them left, right, and center. He managed to reach the walls of Troy, but Apollo dazed him as he tried to scale them. Hector then faced Patroclus, and defeated him in battle, stripping him of his borrowed armor.

Upon hearing the news of Patroclus' death, Achilles threw himself on the ground in a fit of grief. His mother, Thetis, brought him new armor fashioned by Hephaestus, but warned him that if he avenged his friend by killing Hector, that he himself would perish soon after. Nevertheless, Achilles was determined to kill not only Hector, but also as many Trojans as possible. The next morning, he made a formal reconciliation with Agamemnon and entered the battle immediately.

The clash of arms that day was incredible, yet terrible. Hector and Aeneas managed to kill scores of Greeks, but they could not stop Achilles in his revenge-driven fury. In fact, both Aeneas and Hector had to be rescued from Achilles through divine intervention. Throughout the day, Achilles filled the Scamander River so full of bodies that the waters over-flowed and nearly drowned him. The gods, too, engaged in battle among themselves, as Athena felled Ares, Hera boxed Artemis' ears, and Poseidon provoked Apollo.

Eventually, Achilles found Hector outside the walls of Troy. Hector ran from his opponent in fear, circling the city three times. But Athena fooled him into making a stand, and Achilles' lance caught him in the throat. Although Hector had pleaded with Achilles to let his parents ransom his body as he died, Achilles denied him jeeringly. Then, Achilles took Hector's corpse, tied it behind his chariot, and dragged it back to the Greek camp as Hector's wife watched from the walls of Troy.

Patroclus' ghost on the other hand, appeared to Achilles, and demanded a burial. Achilles prepared a glorious funeral for Patroclus. He slit the throats of twelve Trojan nobles as a sacrifice on Patroclus' pyre. After the funeral, there were contests in athletics to honor his friend. For the next eleven days, Achilles dragged Hector's body around the pyre, yet Apollo preserved the corpse from corruption. Then, Zeus instructed Thetis to plead to Achilles to accept the ransom offered by King Priam for Hector's body. Zeus also sent

Hermes to King Priam, and Hermes took the old king safely with his ransom through the Greek lines to Achilles' camp. Achilles treated Priam with courtesy, as Priam reminded him of his own father, Peleus. Achilles took Hector's weight in gold, and in exchange gave Priam the body. Priam took Hector's body back to the city of Troy. During the next eleven days there was an agreed upon truce in the war, as the Trojans mourned for the dead Hector, whom they cremated and buried.

Once the fighting resumed, Achilles managed to kill the Amazon Queen, Penthesileia. When the Trojans brought in Ethiopian reinforcements under Prince Memnon, things became a lot more challenging for the Greeks, and many lost their lives. When the warrior Memnon killed Achilles' friend Antilochus in battle, Achilles retaliated by killing Memnon in a duel. However, Achilles' life was soon to end, as he well knew. One day in battle, Paris shot at Achilles, and the poison arrow, guided by Apollo, connected with him in the right heel, the only place where he was vulnerable. The Greeks had a difficult time retrieving his body from the battlefield. Eventually, Ajax and Odysseus managed to save and retrieve Achilles' body from the Trojans. The Greek hero was given a magnificent funeral.

Shortly after the funeral, an argument arose as to whether Ajax or Odysseus should receive Achilles' powerful armor. The Greek commanders voted on it and the armor was awarded to Odysseus. Furious, Ajax resolved to kill a number of the Greek leaders, including Odysseus. But Athena visited him that night, and afflicted him with madness. During the night, Ajax butchered a number of cattle under the delusion that they were the men who had voted against him. When Athena removed the madness she had inflicted upon him, Ajax realized what he had done, and committed suicide out of shame.

Now Greece was faced with a dire situation. Their two best heroes were dead, which left them anxious about taking Troy. Using brute force had been unsuccessful thus far, and so the Greeks began to turn to the use of oracles. Calchas the oracle informed them that they needed the bow and arrows of Heracles to win the war. These items were currently in the hands of Prince Philoctetes. He was a warrior that the Greeks had abandoned years before on the island of Lemnos whilst heading to Troy, due to him being wounded and failing to heal. Odysseus and Diomedes were sent to Lemnos to fetch the weapons. Once there, Odysseus tricked Philoctetes into handing over the bow and arrows and prepared to leave, but Diomedes offered to take Philoctetes back to Troy with them, where he could be finally cured of his wound. Philoctetes agreed, swallowing his bitterness, and sailed with them for Troy. There, Paris was killed with the arrows of Heracles. Paris might have been spared if his former mistress, the nymph Oenone, had agreed to heal him, but she had refused.

The death of Paris and the possession of Heracles' weapons however did not manage to swing the battle in their favor. Calchas then told the Greeks that only Helenus, the Trojan seer and prince, knew how to defeat Troy. Odysseus proceeded to capture Helenus on Mount Ida. Helenus bore a personal grudge against Troy, having had fought for Helen after Paris died and also having lost her, he was willing to betray his city. First, the Greeks needed to bring Pelops' bones back to Asia from Greece. Agamemnon accomplished this task. Secondly, they needed to bring Achilles' son Neoptolemus into the war, and so a group of Greeks travelled to Scyros to fetch him. Third, the Greeks were instructed to steal the Palladium, a sacred image of Athena, located in the goddess's temple in

Troy. Diomedes and Odysseus took it upon themselves to complete the dangerous mission. Once inside Troy, Odysseus was recognized by Helen, who saw through his disguise but did not give him away. The two heroes seized the sacred image of Athena and escaped unscathed.

Next, the famous Trojan horse entered the story. A great wooden horse was constructed under Greek supervision. The construction had a hollow belly, big enough to hide several soldiers inside. One night, this horse was brought to the Trojan plain, and Greek warriors climbed in under Odysseus' direction. The remaining Greeks burned their camps and sailed off to wait at the nearby island of Tenedos.

The following morning, the Trojans found the Greeks gone and the huge, mysterious horse sitting out the front of Troy. They also came across a Greek named Sinon, whom they took as prisoner. Odysseus had provided Sinon with plausible stories about the Greek departure, the wooden horse, and his own reason for being there. Sinon told Priam and the other Troy soldiers that Athena had deserted the Greeks because of the theft of the Palladium. Without her help they were lost and decided to flee to avoid defeat. But in order to return home safely, they needed a human sacrifice. Sinon told them that he was chosen as the sacrifice, but managed to escape and hide. The horse had been left to placate the angry goddess, and the Greeks were hoping that the Trojans would desecrate it, earning Athena's hatred. These lies were believed by Priam and many Trojans. However, Cassandra and a priest named Laocöon predicted that the horse was full of soldiers. Despite that, nobody believed them. Laöcoon proceeded to hurl a spear at the horse, and in response a hostile god sent two large snakes to strangle him and his sons. The Trojans needed no further proof: they drew the gigantic horse inside their city gates to honor Athena.

That night, the soldiers crept from the horse, killing the sentries. They then opened the gates to let the Greek army in. The Greeks returned and set fires throughout the city. They massacred the inhabitants, and looted. The Trojan resistance was no match. King Priam was slain by Neoptolemus, and by morning all but a few Trojans were dead. Of Trojan males only Aeneas, with his father and son, had escaped the battle. Hector's young son Astyanax was thrown to his death from the walls of the city. The Princess Polyxena, whom Achilles had loved, was sacrificed brutally upon his tomb. Troy was devastated. Hera and Athena had exacted their revenge upon Paris and his city.

Having accomplished their goal in overthrowing Troy, the Greeks now had the challenge of returning back to their various kingdoms. This was not an easy task, as the gods had scores to settle with many Greeks. Soon after the Greeks set sail home, a powerful storm arose that blew much of the Greek fleet far off course.

Of those who travelled by ship, Agamemnon was one of the few that escaped the storm and reached home safely and with ease. But immediately upon his return, his wife, Clytemnestra, and her lover, Aegisthus, murdered him and his followers, including Cassandra, at the banquet table. Clytemnestra was hateful, and had never forgiven her husband for sacrificing Iphigenia.

Menelaus had resolved to murder Helen when he found her in Troy, but upon seeing her naked breasts he lost his motivation, and took her again as his wife. This offended Athena, and Menelaus and Helen and as a result were caught in the storm. They lost most of their ships, and were blown to Crete and Egypt. Unable to return to Sparta because of the winds, Menelaus began trading. Eight years later, he came upon the secret of getting home from the prophetic sea god Proteus, master of changes. Also having had propitiated Athena, Menelaus was allowed to sail to Sparta with Helen, returning a rich man. Upon their eventual deaths, the pair went to the Isles of the Blessed, as favored relations of Zeus.

The less-respected Ajax, who had raped Cassandra in the temple of Athena while plundering Troy, was shipwrecked on his way home. Climbing onto the rocks, he celebrated at having escaped the wrath of the gods. Poseidon saw this, and split the rock to which he clung, drowning him. Athena then began an annual tribute of two maidens from Ajax's fellow Locrians to be sent to Troy.

Extremely resentful of the Greeks, Nauplius caused many of their ships to be destroyed on the Euboean coast by lighting a deceptive beacon. Philoctetes, who also had a grudge against the Greeks for his mistreatment, did not return to Greece but instead sailed to Italy, where he founded two cities.

The prophet Calchas made it to Colophon, where he met the seer Mopsus. He engaged Mopsus in a contest of prophecy, which he lost.

Achilles' son Neoptolemus made himself known as a valiant fighter during the battle of Troy. Warned against ruling his home kingdom, he travelled instead to Epirus, where he became the Molossian King. Neoptolemus proceeded to travel to Delphi where he demanded retribution from Apollo, who had helped kill his father. When the priestess refused his request, he robbed and burned the temple. He later returned again to Delphi, where he was killed in a dispute over sacrificial meat. Apollo's devotees then erected a new temple over his grave.

Of all the Greek soldiers, only the wise Nestor sailed swiftly home and enjoyed the fruits of old age in peace. His virtues of prudence and piety had enabled him to live to see three generations of heroes, and live among his sons for his remaining years.

Chapter 8:
Prometheus

Prometheus (also referred to as Promitheas) was one of the Titans. He was the son of the Titan Iapetus, and Clymene, an Oceanid. He had 2 brothers, Epimetheus, Atlas and Menoetius. His name is derived from the Greek word meaning 'forethought'.

During the war between the Titans and the Olympian gods, Prometheus sided with Zeus, assisting him in overthrowing the old gods. Being on the winning side, Prometheus avoided being punished for his actions, along with the rest of the Titans and was therefore not sent to Tartarus, the Underworld.

Prometheus was known as the the protector and benefactor of mankind. He once tricked Zeus by asking him to choose between two gifts; beef hidden inside an ox's stomach (something pleasing hidden inside a repelling exterior) or bones wrapped in glistening fat (something inedible hidden inside a pleasing exterior). Zeus chose the latter option, and as a result a precedent was created as to what humans could sacrifice from then onwards. So, humans began to keep the meat for themselves and only sacrificed bones to the gods.

As a result of this trick, Zeus was infuriated. Zeus then decided to hide fire from humans as a form of punishment. Prometheus of course, wanted to help humankind. In an attempt to help, he managed to steal fire and give it to the humans. This only enraged Zeus, and as you discovered earlier, he asked Hephaestus to create Pandora, the first woman.

According to Hesiod, Pandora would bring great trouble to mankind. Zeus also punished Prometheus by having him chained to a rock, where an eagle ate his liver during the day, and the liver was regenerated during the night due to Prometheus' immortality. It was intended for Prometheus to suffer for eternity, but fortunately for him he was later saved by the demigod Hercules.

Chapter 9:
Hyacinthus

Hyacinthus (also known as Hyacinth) was a young, handsome Spartan Prince. Hyacinthus was a great friend, and also lover of the god Apollo.

One day, whilst walking upon a hillside, Apollo saw another shepherd boy, who was playing music on a pipe. Apollo was attracted by his music, and headed towards him. As Apollo drew near, he stopped and stood before the shepherd, asking " What is thy name, noble youth?". The shepherd was stunned by the brightness emanating from the god, but responded simply. " Hyacinthus". Apollo then asked Hyacinthus if he could use his pipe to play some music of his own.

Hyacinthus was amazed at the incredible beauty of Apollo, but was even more awestruck by the sound of his music, as it was like nothing a mortal had ever heard before. Hyacinthus stood and watched silently in awe. Apollo finally finished playing, and handed back the pipe, saying frankly, "I like you, Hyacinthus.' We will be friends, and you shall go with me to the palace of King Admetus."

Hyacinthus' eyes lit up; he badly wanted to go, but thinking of his duties as a shepherd, he said, " But what would become of my sheep? I must not leave them. No, no, Apollo; I cannot go with you!? " Noble youth, I love you the better because you prefer duty to pleasure; and since you cannot come with me, I will come to you. Tomorrow I will come again". True to his word, Apollo returned again; and for many long days they played, talked, and learned to love one another.

Their relationship was beautiful, and they continue to spend many days together. Unfortunately, that all ended on one fateful day when they were playing a game of discus. Hyacinthus wished that Apollo would win the game, and Apollo wished for the success of Hyacinthus.

Apollo picked up the discus, and performed a powerful throw. He would have won, but The West Wind intervened. The West Wind is a wild and gloomy fellow, and had grown jealous of their beautiful friendship. Thinking that his actions would make them quarrel, he changed the direction of the wind. The discus was blown forcefully so that it bounded back and hit Hyacinthus on the forehead, knocking him to the ground. In other versions of the story, Hyacinthus attempted to impress Apollo by trying to catch the discus, and was instead, struck in the head.

Either way, Hyacinthus took a mighty blow to the head, taking both him and Apollo by surprise. Apollo rushed toward his friend, and lifted his wounded head from the ground. Hyacinthus however was unresponsive, and his head drooped like a broken flower. Apollo wept and moaned, for Hyacinthus had died instantly from the impact. He had instantly lost his beloved friend in such a cruel and unpredictable way.

"Ah, Hyacinthus, would that I could have died for thee. My lyre shall tell of thy sad fate, and I will cause thee to be remembered, for thou art indeed a noble friend" said Apollo to his fallen companion.

Where the blood of Hyacinthus had fallen, Apollo caused to spring up the beautiful flower which bears his name, the hyacinth.

And such is the story of Hyacinthus, and of course the reason why the hyacinth flower we know today has it's name.

Chapter 10:
Procne & Philomena

Pandion, the King of Athens, married his maternal Aunt, Zeuxippe. Together, they had two daughters, Procne and Philomela, and also twin sons, Erechtheus and Butes. Pandion however, wasn't a great father, and was constantly preoccupied with his kingdom. When Athens went to war with Abdacus, Pandion called upon his neighbor Tereus who resided in Thrace, and asked for his help.

Tereus was not only the ruler of Daulis, he was also the son of Ares. Thanks to his many connections in Thrace, he won the war for Pandion. Pandion, being a diplomat and smart businessman, decided that Tereus should be well rewarded. He also aimed to consolidate a relationship with him, and since he was a horrible father who saw his daughters primarily as bargaining tools, gave his daughter Procne to Tereus to be his wife.

Tereus had his way with Procne, leaving her alone to take care of their son, Itys. After she was impregnated however, Tereus abandoned Procne in his house out in the country, telling nobody of her whereabouts. Then, he went to the home of Pandion, with his eyes set on Philomela. He lied to Philomela, telling her that her sister had died. He proceeded to seduce Philomela, and soon thereafter, they were married.

Upon marrying her, Tereus cut Philomena's tongue out. Philomela however, was an accomplished weaver (like many upper class Greek women were), and she wove characters into a robe in order to communicate to her sister. Once she realized that Procne was in fact alive, she sent the robe to her to let Procne know what was going on. Procne, who had until that moment been oblivious to what had happened, immediately set out to get her revenge, bringing her son, Itys, with her. Eventually, Procne found her sister, but due to her own abuse and also what she saw had been done to her sister, Procne went crazy.

Procne pretended to play along with Tereus' evilness, and told him that she would make him a magnificent dinner. She then went into the back room, where she killed her son Itys. She proceeded to boil him up, and served him to Tereus. While Tereus unknowingly feasted on his own son, Procne grabbed Philomela and ran.

Once Tereus realized that the sisters had disappeared, he took an axe and went after them. The women ran, but they were not making much ground. They prayed to the Gods to be turned into birds, and the Gods took pity upon them. Procne was transformed into the nightingale, constantly crying her sorrow in the sounds, "Itu, Itu" (the name of her son). Philomela became the voiceless swallow. Tereus was also changed into a bird, and became the hoopoe, which calls out, "pou, pou" which means "where, where" in Greek.

Chapter 11:
Oedipus

Oedipus was the King of the city of Thebes. He was the son of King Laius and Queen Jocasta. Unknowingly, he married his mother and together they had four children; Polynices, Eteocles, Antigone, and Ismene.

It all began when King Laius consulted the Oracle at Delphi to ask if he and his wife would ever have children. The prophecy given was that any son that was born out of their union would kill them. Eventually, Jocasta fell pregnant and gave birth to a son. To avoid the prophecy from playing out, Laius ordered his servants to pierce the baby's ankles, so that he would not be able to crawl; that's how the baby got the name Oedipus, meaning swollen foot. Jocasta then gave the baby to one of their shepherds, instructing him to leave the baby in the mountains to die. Unable to bring himself to do this, the shepherd handed the baby over to another shepherd, who then brought it to the court of King Polybus and Queen Merope of Corinth.

The royal couple, also childless, decided to adopt the poor baby and raise him as their own. When Oedipus grew up, someone informed him of the truth; that Polybus and Merope were not his actual parents. Wanting to find the truth, he decided to investigate this matter. On his quest, Oedipus ended up in Delphi, to consult the Oracle. There, the Oracle told him that he would kill his father and marry his mother. Upon hearing this, Oedipus thought that the prophecy meant Polybus and Merope, and to avoid it he decided not to return to Corinth. Instead, he began to head towards the city of Thebes, where his biological parents lived.

During his journey towards Thebes, he crossed paths with King Laius, his biological father, who was on a chariot heading towards the Oracle once again. Oedipus and Laius' charioteer argued over who had the right of way. Not knowing that the King was in fact his father, the quarrel ended up with Oedipus killing not only the charioteer, but also his father. This, fulfilled the first part of the prophecy.

Later on his trip, he met a monster called Sphinx, who plagued the region of Thebes, destroying crops and killing travelers who did not correctly provide the answer its questions. The Sphinx asked Oedipus the same question it asked the rest; 'what walks on four feet in the morning, two in the afternoon, and three at night?' Previously, nobody had correctly answered the question, and the Sphinx had slain and devoured all of them. Oedipus carefully contemplated the question, and eventually became the first to give the correct answer; 'man, who crawls on all fours as a baby, he walks on two legs as an adult, and needs a walking stick when old.' The Sphinx was in disbelief that its difficult riddle had been solved, and in shock, fell off of the rock it was perched upon, hitting its head on the way down and dying.

When Oedipus finally arrived at Thebes, he was accepted graciously by Creon, Jocasta's brother and his uncle. Creon had been serving as the temporary king after Laius' death. Creon had declared that any man killed the Sphinx would be named as the new King, and would have Jocasta as a wife. This, of course fulfilled the second part of the prophecy. Oedipus rose to the throne of Thebes, unknowingly marrying his mother.

Together, Oedipus and Jocasta had four children; Eteocles, Polynices, Antigone, and Ismene. Many years later, pestilence was brought upon the city of Thebes. In response, Oedipus sent his Uncle Creon to the Oracle at Delphi to receive consultation. Creon was informed that the pestilence was caused because the killer of Laius had not been brought to justice. Oedipus cursed the killer of Laius, and demanded of the prophet Tiresias to know who the killer was. Tiresias revealed that it was in fact Oedipus who killed the former king, and also that he did not know who his true parents were. This information was brought back to the court, where Oedipus and Creon got into a heated debate. Jocasta intervened in the argument, recounting the story of her son and how he had supposedly died.

At that very moment, a messenger from Corinth entered itno the court and explained to everyone that Polybus had died. Oedipus was initially relieved, believing that Polybus was his biological father, and that the prophecy had not come true. Oedipus however, said that he would not attend the funeral, in order to avoid meeting his mother and maybe causing the second part of the prophecy to play out. The messenger then confirmed to him that he was in fact adopted, and that Polybus and Merope were not his real parents.

In this moment, Oedipus had a revelation. He suddenly realized that he had in fact killed his father years ago, and that he had married his mother, fulfilling the prophecy. Oedipus searched for Jocasta, who had disappeared moments earlier. He found her body shortly thereafter, having hung herself after coming to the same realization that he had. Oedipus then took a brooch from her gown, and using the pin, he stabbed his eyes, blinding himself. He then fled from the city, guided by his daughter Antigone. They travelled to the court of King Theseus of Athens, where they were both welcomed with open arms. He spent his days there, before eventually passing away.

Following Oedipus' death, his sons Polynices and Eteocles chose to share the throne. Eteocles took his turn first, but then refused to give up the throne when his time was over. In response, Polynices left Thebes and returned with an army. This led to a war, referred to as 'Seven Against Thebes'. In the fight, both brothers were unsuccessful in winning the throne, as both died on the battlefield.

Chapter 12:
Pygmalion & Galatea

On the island of Cyprus, lived Pygmalion, a young and extremely talented sculptor.

Pygmalion was somewhat of a woman-hater. He struggled to see the great aspects of women, and instead only took note of their multiple flaws. So it's no surprise that he resolved to never marry, and instead to focus and devote his life to his art.

Ironically enough, the masterpiece upon which he exercised the full extent of his skill was the sculpture of a woman. Perhaps, it was the result of his desire to create the perfect woman, a yardstick by which all the living women he encountered could be measured by.

For whatever reason, Pygmalion made use of all of his talent on this piece, like no other artwork he had previously created. The result was absolutely stunning, a truly beautiful work of art. Despite it's incredible design, he wasn't quite satisfied with his work. Pygmalion demanded perfection. He continued working on his female magnum opus, laboring daily, untiringly, unrelentingly, until he reached this ideal.

When at last, he was finished, the result was a wonder to behold. His piece was incomparable, for it did not even resemble a work of art. His sculptured beauty was so lifelike, at a glance she could have been mistaken for real flesh and blood.

Her beauty was unparalleled. No sculpture ever made—indeed no woman ever born—could rival her.

In the moment of her completion, womankind had their revenge upon the scornful young man, for Pygmalion had fallen in love. He had fallen in love deeply, passionately, *inexplicably*, with his very own creation.

It was a difficult emotion for Pygmalion to understand, for his beloved was an inanimate, lifeless thing and incapable of reciprocation—never able to kiss him, to grasp his hand, to smile, to laugh, to flush with emotion, to respond to his desire—and yet, he could not stop himself from loving her.

At first, he simply played a game of make-believe, just like a child would: he dressed her in fancy gowns, presented her with gifts, put her to bed at night and tucked her in. He would vividly imagine her reactions, and imagine how she would respond when he spoke to her; but in the end, it was never enough. He knew that he was hopelessly in love with a creation that could never possibly love him back.

Of course, the love Pygmalion expressed did not escape the attention of the goddess of love herself; none other than Aphrodite.

Pygmalion captured Aphrodite's attention, as he was a new kind of lover, afflicted by desire as so many lovers are, and yet so entirely different than the rest. He was simply *original*. It became Aphrodite's aim to help him out.

Cyprus, Pygmalion's home, was particularly fond of Aphrodite. It was the island that first welcomed her when she rose out of the sea foam. As such, her feast day was especially honored there. Incredible numbers of people crowded her temples, bringing gifts for her, and pleading for the goddess of love to give them success in romance.

Pygmalion attended also, but what could he possibly have asked for? He knew that it would be impossible for his masterpiece to love him back, and so he instead prayed that he might find a maiden *similar* to her, if that were even possible.

However, Aphrodite knew the true desire of his heart and as a sign of her favor, she made the flame of the altar in front of him leap three times. Pygmalion returned home, thoughtful of this good omen.

When he arrived home, he immediately went to find his beloved. Thinking of the omen at Aphrodite's altar, he gently caressed her and was startled in surprise—she was warm to his touch!

Doubting what he had felt, he gave her a long, lingering kiss. To his amazement and utter disbelief, he felt her cold lips grow soft and warm under his. He felt her transform as he held her: the rigidness of her limbs vanished and she softened to the touch as the stone she was carved from turned to flesh.

He held her wrists and marveled at her pulse, warm and beating under his fingertips. At last, his joy was complete, as he looked at her face and saw her smile timidly at him, her cheeks dusted pink by a maiden's innocent blush.

Pygmalion knew then what Aphrodite had done for him and his happiness and gratitude was beyond words.

Pygmalion named the maiden Galatea, and Aphrodite herself attended their wedding. Their son was named Paphos, and the goddess's favorite city was named after him.

Chapter 13:
Homer

Being a person who is interested in Greek mythology, it is most likely that you have heard of Homer before.

Homer was a Greek poet, responsible for two major works detailing Greek mythological stories, namely: The Iliad, and The Odyssey.

Homer is believed to have been born sometime between 750 and 1200 BC, somewhere along the coast of Asia Minor.

Not much is known of Homer, other than his incredible impact on Western culture as a result of his poems. Some scholars in fact, debate whether Homer was just one man, or rather a group of people.

Homer is the earliest poet in Western history whose works have survived up until modern day. This is even more amazing given the fact that Homer did not write down his work, and rather it was recited from memory. Stories and poems during Homer's time were simply transmitted orally, and story-telling was a large part of the culture. His poems were not actually written down until much later.

Today, English-translated versions of Homer's poems can be purchased as a physical book, or can be downloaded digitally for free. They are quite large and detailed, and are one of the biggest reasons that Greek mythology has continued to influence our culture thousands of years since its inception.

The Iliad

The Iliad was Homer's first piece of work. It is composed of 15,693 lines of verse, and is divided into 24 individual books (one for each letter of the Greek alphabet).

The poem covers the topic of the Trojan war, and is set during the final year of the 10-year battle. The poem is named after the city of Troy, which is also known as 'Ilium'.

The Odyssey

The Odyssey is Homer's sequel to the Iliad. Slightly shorter than his first work, the Odyssey consists of 12,109 lines of verse. Just like The Iliad, it is broken down into 24 separate books.

The poem focuses primarily on Odysseus (whom the poem is named after), and his journey home after the Trojan war had ended. Odysseus faced many setbacks during his venture home, including godly intervention thanks to Poseidon, and encounters with the Sirens and the Cyclops. The poem also details the slaying of his wife Penelope's suitors upon his return home to Ithaca.

Not much at all is known about Homer, where he was born, what period of time he was alive, or if he was even just one man at all! Regardless, he is easily one of the main reasons that Greek mythology is so widely-known about today. I would highly recommend taking a look at his incredible poems, available for free download on Amazon.

Conclusion

Thanks again for taking the time to read this book!

You should now have a good knowledge of Greek Mythology, and the incredible stories and myths of the different heroes, gods, and monsters!

If you enjoyed this book, please take the time to leave me a review on Amazon. I appreciate your honest feedback, and it really helps me to continue producing high quality books.

Made in the USA
Lexington, KY
26 January 2017